The Eternal Journey:

Preparing for the Life to Come

A Guide to the Hereafter, Signs of the Hour, and the Path to Paradise

Compiled and Edited by

Hussein Elasrag

Published by Hussein Elasrag

"This work is inspired by the Quran and authentic Sunnah, drawing from traditional Islamic teachings to remind believers of the transient nature of this world and the eternal rewards of the Hereafter."

In The Eternal Journey, Hussein Elasrag offers a profound exploration of the Islamic perspective on the Hereafter. From the fleeting reality of this world to the trials of the grave, the signs of the Hour, and the unimaginable beauties of Paradise, this book serves as a spiritual compass for modern Muslims. Compiled from the Quran and Sahih Hadith, it calls readers to reflect, repent, and prepare for the ultimate return to Allah. Ideal for seekers of faith and knowledge.

The Eternal Journey: Preparing for the Life to Come

A Guide to the Hereafter, Signs of the Hour, and the Path to Eternal Bliss

Compiled and Edited by

Hussein Elasrag

Dedication

To every soul seeking the light of faith in a world of fleeting shadows—may this journey lead you to the eternal gardens of Paradise.

Foreword

In the hustle of modern life, where technology connects us across continents yet often leaves us feeling more isolated, the call to reflect on the Hereafter rings louder than ever. This book is not merely a recounting of ancient prophecies or divine warnings; it is a roadmap for the contemporary believer. Drawing from the timeless wisdom of the Quran and the authentic Sunnah, we explore the transient nature of this world, the inevitability of death, the trials that await, and the boundless rewards of the life to come. As we navigate the challenges of 2025—global uncertainties, moral decays, and spiritual voids—this guide reminds us that true fulfillment lies not in material pursuits but in preparing for the eternal. Let these pages stir your heart, ignite your faith, and inspire action. For as the Prophet Muhammad (peace be upon him) said, "The smart one is he who subdues his soul and works for what comes after death" (Tirmidhi). May Allah guide us all to the straight path.

Hussein Elasrag

Chapter 1: The Fleeting Nature of This World

We, the human family dwelling upon this blue planet, often harbor a profound illusion: that this earthly existence is our true home, a permanent abode where we can anchor our dreams, build empires, and linger indefinitely. Yet, the divine revelation shatters this mirage, unveiling a stark reality. Life in this world—dunya—is but a brief interlude, a transient station on an inexorable journey toward the ultimate destination: the Hereafter (Akhirah). Imagine our lives as passengers on a grand, cosmic train, hurtling through veiled landscapes toward an unseen terminus. Each carriage represents a phase: the womb's nine-month sanctuary, where we first draw breath in darkness; the vibrant yet ephemeral dunya, alive with joys and trials; and finally, the eternal realms of Paradise or Hellfire. The Prophet Muhammad (peace be upon him) captured this essence beautifully: "Be in this world as if you were a stranger or a wayfarer" (Sahih Bukhari). He himself exemplified this detachment, mending his sandals while seated on the pulpit, a reminder that even the greatest of creation viewed dunya as a mere pitstop. Our "ticket" for this voyage bears three coupons. The first is severed at birth, marking the end of prenatal peace. The second tears away at death, closing the chapter of worldly endeavors. The last remains for the reckoning—torn in bliss or torment, determining our forever. The Quran echoes this truth: "Every soul will taste death.

Then to Us will you be returned" (Surah Al-Ankabut 29:57). In an era of rapid change—where algorithms dictate our days and screens eclipse our nights—this reminder is vital. Consider the billionaire chasing endless wealth or the influencer curating a facade of perfection; both are wayfarers, unaware that time devours all illusions. Why does this matter? Because recognizing dunya's impermanence liberates us from its chains. The Prophet (peace be upon him) warned his companions against over-attachment: "I do not fear poverty for you, but I fear that you will compete for this world as those before you did, and it will destroy you as it destroyed them" (Sahih Muslim). History bears witness: the mighty Pharaohs, buried with treasures, now dust; the opulent cities of 'Ad and Thamud, reduced to ruins by divine decree. Today, in 2025, we see echoes—nations gripped by economic turmoil, societies fractured by moral decay—yet the believer stands firm, investing in deeds that transcend time. To embrace this perspective, pause amid your daily rush: What if this moment were your last? Use it to recite a verse, give charity, or mend a tie. As Ibn al-Qayyim reflected, "The world is a bridge; cross it, but do not build upon it." In the chapters ahead, we delve deeper: the soul's departure, the grave's solitude, the Hour's signs, and Paradise's splendor. May this journey awaken your soul to the eternal call.

Chapter 2: The Inevitability of Death

Death is not a distant specter lurking in the shadows of old age; it is the unyielding companion of every breath we take, the silent architect of our finite existence. In the Quran, Allah reminds us with profound simplicity: "Every soul will taste death. Then to Us will you be returned" (Surah Al-Ankabut 29:57). This verse is not a mere philosophical musing but a divine certainty, a call to awaken from the slumber of denial that grips so many in our fast-paced world.Consider the rhythm of modern life in 2025: endless notifications, virtual meetings that blur into nights, and a culture that glorifies youth and vitality. We scroll through feeds of flawless lives, postponing reflections on mortality until "someday." Yet, the Prophet Muhammad (peace be upon him) shattered such illusions early in his mission. When questioned about the Hour, he replied, "What have you prepared for it?" (Sahih Bukhari). Death, then, is not the end but the gateway—the moment when the veil lifts, and our deeds are laid bare.The inevitability of death humbles the mighty and equalizes the races. Empires crumble, fortunes dissipate, and the most influential voices fall silent. As the Prophet (peace be upon him) taught, "The life of man is of three days: what has passed is gone, what is to come is not yet, and the present day is a provision—a traveler benefits from it, but he does not stay" (Ibn Hibban). In an age of medical miracles that extend life, we must remember: no technology can outrun the angel of death, Azrael, who seizes souls by Allah's command.To embrace this truth is to live with purpose. It prompts us to audit our days: Are we amassing wealth at the expense of worship? Chasing fleeting relationships while neglecting the ties of faith? The early companions exemplified this; Abu Bakr (may Allah be pleased with him) wept at the thought of death, not from fear, but from longing for the meeting with his Lord. Let us, too, make death a frequent visitor in our thoughts, transforming routine moments into acts of eternal value.

Chapter 3: The Agony of Death (Sakarat al-Mawt)

The throes of death—known in Arabic as Sakarat al-Mawt—are among the most poignant descriptions in Islamic eschatology, a moment of profound trial where the soul confronts its separation from the body. The Quran paints this scene vividly: "And the agony of death will come in truth; that is what you used to avoid" (Surah Qaf 50:19). It is the ultimate equalizer, stripping away pretenses and revealing the heart's true state.Imagine the scene: the room grows dim, loved ones gather in hushed prayer, and the body, once vibrant, now trembles under an invisible weight. The soul clings to its vessel, but the angels descend—gentle for the believer, severe for the disbeliever. For the righteous, it is like the extraction of a wet wool thread from dry, with ease and mercy (Sahih Bukhari). The Prophet (peace be upon him) described it: "Death is the first station of the Hereafter; when the believer is dying, the angels of mercy descend with white silk, saying, 'O soul at peace, come out to the forgiveness of Allah and His pleasure'" (Ahmad).Yet, for the heedless, it is torment: the soul resists, the chest tightens, and regrets flood like a storm. The disbeliever sees the angels of punishment, their faces darkened, wrapping the soul in coarse cloth (Sahih Muslim). In our time, where distractions abound—social media debates, endless work hours—this agony serves as a wake-up call. What if, in your final moments, your mind races not to loved ones, but to missed prayers or unspoken apologies? The Prophet (peace be upon him) urged: "When you bury one of your dead, do not say, 'O so-and-so,' but say, 'O one who has been taken to Allah'" (Tirmidhi), reminding us that death is personal, intimate, and divine.The agony underscores a key lesson: preparation is key. Recite the Shahadah daily, forgive readily, and seek Allah's mercy. As contemporary scholars note, in an era of pandemics and uncertainties, Sakarat al-Mawt teaches resilience—face trials in life with the grace that eases the final one.

Chapter 4: The Benefits of Remembering Death

To remember death is not to dwell in gloom but to ignite a flame of vigilance, transforming ordinary lives into purposeful quests. The Prophet Muhammad (peace be upon him) said, "Increase your remembrance of the destroyer of pleasures" (Tirmidhi), referring to death as the great equalizer that dissolves worldly delights. This practice, known as Dhikr al-Mawt, is a spiritual discipline praised in the Sunnah for its profound rewards.First, it fosters detachment from dunya's illusions. In a world obsessed with accumulation—stocks rising, trends fleeting—recalling death curbs greed and envy. The companions of the Prophet (peace be upon him) would visit graves weekly, emerging with softened hearts, as if they had conversed with the departed. Abu Hurairah (may Allah be pleased with him) narrated that the Prophet (peace be upon him) passed by a grave and said, "If I were to command anyone to prostrate to another, I would command a son to prostrate to his father, but prostration is only due to Allah" (Muslim)—a reminder of humility before the inevitable.Second, it accelerates repentance (Tawbah). The Quran warns: "The time for repentance has passed for them" (Surah An-Nisa 4:18), yet remembering death opens the door wide. In 2025, amid digital addictions and moral relativism, this dhikr acts as an antidote—prompting us to log off screens for salah, reconcile with family, or give sadaqah before it's too late. The Prophet (peace be upon him) emphasized: "The one who remembers death often is the one who prepares best for it" (Ibn Majah).Third, it cultivates gratitude and presence. By envisioning life's end, we savor blessings: a child's laugh, a shared iftar, the adhan's echo. Umar ibn al-Khattab (may Allah be pleased with him) advised, "Take account of yourselves before you are taken to account," leading to a life of balanced deeds. Modern psychology echoes this—studies on mortality salience show it boosts empathy and purpose—yet Islam offers the eternal framework.Finally, it promises divine reward. The Prophet (peace be upon him) said, "The one who remembers death twenty times a day will be protected from the punishment of the grave" (Tabarani). In practice, integrate it: reflect during commute, visit a cemetery monthly, or end prayers with, "O Allah, let me taste the sweetness of faith before death claims me."In these benefits lies a call to action: let death's shadow illuminate your path, turning fear into fuel for faith. As we move to the grave's solitude, remember—preparation today ensures peace tomorrow.

Chapter 5: The Solitude of the Grave

The grave—Qabr in Arabic—is not merely a plot of earth where the body rests; it is the first dwelling of the Hereafter, a narrow chamber that echoes with the soul's solitude and the echoes of one's deeds. Following death's final breath, the believer (or disbeliever) is lowered into this earthen embrace, and the world above fades into irrelevance. The Prophet Muhammad (peace be upon him) described it starkly: "The grave is either a garden from the gardens of Paradise or a pit from the pits of Hell" (Tirmidhi). This bifurcation underscores a pivotal truth: the grave is the bridge between dunya and the grand assembly of Judgment.Upon burial, the grave constricts around the body, testing the soul's resolve. For the righteous, it expands into a verdant meadow, fragrant with mercy, where angels greet with glad tidings. The Quran alludes to this transition: "And if you could but see when the angels take those who have wronged themselves [with their hands] and say, 'In what [condition] were you?' They will say, 'We were oppressed in the land.' They [the angels] will say, 'Was not My earth sufficient for you to take refuge therein?'" (Surah Ibrahim 14:21). Yet, this is but a prelude; the true essence lies in what follows—the questioning and trials that define the grave's occupant.In our era of perpetual connectivity—where even solitude is interrupted by pings and posts—the grave's isolation is a profound shock. No Wi-Fi, no notifications, no distractions; only the self confronts the divine ledger. Imagine a tech executive, buried amid gadgets, now facing the silence that amplifies every neglected prayer. This solitude is mercy for the prepared soul, a time for reflection before the greater trials. As the Prophet (peace be upon him) advised, "Seek refuge with Allah from the punishment of the grave" (Sahih Bukhari), urging us to fortify our graves with deeds in life.The grave, then, is a mirror: it reflects the heart's purity or corruption. For the believer, it becomes a place of rest, awaiting the resurrection's trumpet. For others, a foretaste of regret. Let this chapter stir you to action—visit graves not as tourists, but as pilgrims seeking lessons in humility.

Chapter 6: Trials in the Grave (Fitnat al-Qabr)

The trials of the grave—Fitnat al-Qabr—are among the most harrowing stages of the soul's journey, a private inquisition where two angels, Munkar and Nakir, descend to question the deceased. With voices like thunder and eyes like lightning, they demand: "Who is your Lord? What is your religion? Who is your prophet?" (Sunan Abi Dawud). The grave, once a quiet tomb, transforms into a courtroom of the unseen, where answers determine comfort or constriction.For the believer, the response flows effortlessly: "My Lord is Allah, my religion is Islam, and my prophet is Muhammad (peace be upon him)." The angels affirm, "We knew you would say that," and the grave widens into bliss

(Sahih Bukhari). Light fills the space, and the soul glimpses Paradise's gates, sustained by deeds like charity and Quran recitation. The Prophet (peace be upon him) reassured: "When the believer is questioned in his grave, Allah strengthens his heart, and he answers correctly" (Ibn Majah).Conversely, the disbeliever or hypocrite stammers, "Alas! I do not know," triggering the grave's squeeze—a crushing embrace that fractures ribs and evokes screams unheard above ground. The Quran warns of such reckoning: "The Fire will burn their faces, and they therein will have taut smiles" (Surah Al-Mu'minun 23:104). In 2025, amid rising atheism and moral ambiguity, these trials highlight the peril of superficial faith. A social media "Muslim" who posts quotes but skips Fajr may falter here, their hypocrisy exposed in isolation.These trials test three pillars: Tawhid (oneness of God), Risalah (prophethood), and the believer's deeds. The Prophet (peace be upon him) said, "The grave speaks to the believer: 'Welcome, may Allah make you prosper.' It expands sixty cubits and fills with light" (Musnad Ahmad). To prepare, fortify with nightly dhikr and sincere deeds—acts that echo in the grave's silence. As contemporary challenges like mental health crises remind us, true peace begins with spiritual readiness; the grave's trial is but an extension of life's unseen struggles.

Chapter 7: Salvation from the Punishment of the Grave

What shields the soul from the grave's torment? Salvation lies not in worldly status or rituals alone, but in a heart anchored in faith and deeds that endure. The Prophet Muhammad (peace be upon him) outlined clear paths: "Seek refuge from the punishment of the grave, for it is the first stage of the Hereafter" (Sahih Bukhari). This supplication, recited in every prayer's tashahhud, is our first line of defense.Key safeguards include:

- Surah Al-Mulk's Recitation: The Prophet (peace be upon him) said, "Surah Tabarak al-Mulk protects from the punishment of the grave; it intercedes for its reciter until forgiven" (Tirmidhi). Recite it nightly; in a world of insomnia from screens, let its verses be your lullaby of protection.

■ Constant Dhikr and Tawhid: Angels record the believer's affirmations, easing the questioning. As the Prophet (peace be upon him) taught, "The best words are four: Subhan Allah, Alhamdulillah, La ilaha illallah, Allahu Akbar" (Sahih Muslim). In 2025's chaos—wars, economic woes—these become anchors, ensuring the grave's expansion.

■ Charity and Good Deeds: Sadaqah Jariyah (ongoing charity, like building a mosque or teaching knowledge) continues benefiting post-death. The Prophet (peace be upon him) said, "When the son of Adam dies, his deeds cease except for three: ongoing charity, beneficial knowledge, or a righteous child who prays for him" (Sahih Muslim).

■ Avoiding Major Sins: Shun riba, zina, and backbiting, for they invite squeezing. The Quran cautions: "Fear a Day when no soul will avail another" (Surah Al-Baqarah 2:48).

Who are the saved? Primarily the steadfast believers: martyrs (shuhada), Quran reciters, and those who died in prostration (Ibn Majah). Even sinners may find respite through intercession. In today's context, where anxiety plagues millions, salvation teaches proactive faith—turn trials into tawbah, ensuring the grave becomes a garden, not a prison.As we conclude this stage, reflect: What deed will widen your grave? The journey continues to the Hour's signs—may Allah grant us ease therein.

Chapter 8: The Minor Signs of the Hour – An Introduction

The Hour (As-Sa'ah)—the Day of Judgment—is not a vague prophecy but a divinely ordained event preceded by unmistakable signs, divided into minor (sughra) and major (kubra). The minor signs are like the early tremors before an earthquake, subtle yet cumulative warnings that the end draws near. The Prophet Muhammad (peace be upon him) said, "The Hour will not be established until... [a list of signs unfolds]" (Sahih Bukhari), enumerating over fifty indicators that we witness unfolding across centuries.These signs serve multiple purposes: to test faith, urge repentance, and affirm the truth of revelation. In the Quran, Allah declares, "Do they then wait for anything other than that the angels should come to them or that your Lord should come, or that some of the signs of your Lord should come [like the Day of Resurrection]?" (Surah Al-An'am 6:158). Unlike the major signs—cataclysmic events like the emergence of the Dajjal—the minor ones are societal and moral shifts, often gradual, allowing time for reflection.In 2025, as global interconnectedness accelerates moral erosion through algorithms promoting vice and echo chambers fueling division, these signs feel eerily relevant. They are not mere curiosities but calls to action: examine your society, your heart, and realign with the Sunnah. The Prophet (peace be upon him) emphasized their progression: "The Hour will come upon the worst of people" (Musnad Ahmad), a sobering reminder that unchecked trends lead to ruin. Over the next chapters, we explore these signs in detail, drawing from authentic narrations to discern patterns and prepare accordingly. May Allah grant us insight to recognize and respond.

Chapter 9: Key Minor Signs – Moral and Social Decay

Among the minor signs, several highlight the erosion of moral fabric, serving as divine diagnostics of a society's spiritual health. These are not abstract; they mirror the Prophet's (peace be upon him) warnings, validated by history and our present.

1- The Appearance of False Prophets: The Prophet (peace be upon him) foretold, "There will be thirty liars among my Ummah, each claiming to be a prophet, but I am the seal of the prophets" (Sahih Bukhari). These impostors deceive with charisma, twisting scripture for gain. In the 20th century, figures like Mirza Ghulam Ahmad (Ahmadiyya founder) and others emerged; today, in 2025, social media amplifies "spiritual influencers" peddling syncretic faiths or doomsday cults, luring the vulnerable. The lesson: cling to the Quran and Sunnah as your anchor, verifying claims against authentic sources.

2- The Spread of False Peace and Complacency: "Peace" becomes a hollow slogan, masking underlying chaos. The hadith states, "The Hour will not come until people greet with 'Peace' but mean it not" (Sahih Muslim). In our era of diplomatic facades and performative allyship on global stages, true aman (security) eludes us amid wars and cyber threats. This sign urges sincerity: offer salam with heart, fostering genuine community bonds.

3- The Fire in Hijaz and Wars with the Turks: A great fire will erupt in Hijaz (modern Saudi Arabia), visible from Busra (Syria), as per the

Prophet (peace be upon him) (Sahih Bukhari). Historically linked to events like the 654 CE eruption, it symbolizes turmoil in the heartland of Islam. Likewise, conflicts with "the Turks" (interpreted as Central Asian powers) point to geopolitical strife. In 2025, with rising tensions in the Middle East and Eurasian alliances, these remind us to pray for ummah's unity, avoiding blind nationalism.

4- Loss of Trust and the Rise of Ignorance: "When trust is lost, the Hour has come" (Sahih Bukhari). Amanah (trustworthiness) vanishes as contracts break and leaders betray. Knowledge subsides while ignorance prevails: scholars diminish, replaced by unqualified voices. Today, fake news and AI-generated misinformation erode truth; the Prophet (peace be upon him) said, "Knowledge will be taken away by the death of scholars, and ignorance will spread" (Sahih Bukhari). Counter this by seeking ilm from reliable sources and embodying honesty in dealings.

5- The Proliferation of Security Forces and Prevailing Zina: Armies of police and guards multiply, a sign of societal breakdown (Sunan Ibn Majah). Zina (fornication) becomes rampant, normalized through media. In 2025, surveillance states and dating apps exemplify this—yet the Quran commands, "And come not near to unlawful sexual intercourse" (Surah Al-Isra 17:32). The remedy: lower gazes, uphold modesty, and promote chaste marriages.

6- The Spread of Riba and Lavish Mosques: Usury (riba) permeates economies, from crypto loans to high-interest debts, fulfilling "Riba will spread" (Sahih Muslim). Mosques become ornate spectacles, yet hearts distant from prayer. The Prophet (peace be upon him) warned against extravagance: "Allah does not look at your forms or wealth, but at your hearts and deeds" (Sahih Muslim). Build faith, not facades.

7- Tall Buildings, Slave Mothers Birthing Masters, and Widespread Bloodshed: Skyscrapers symbolize hubris, as "Shepherds compete in building tall structures" (Sahih Bukhari)—think Dubai's Burj Khalifa amid inequality. The paradox of a slave woman birthing her mistress (Sunan Abi Dawud) reflects social inversion, like modern gig economies where the poor serve the elite's heirs.

Bloodshed surges: "Killing will increase" (Sahih Bukhari), seen in urban violence and conflicts.

These signs, unfolding like a tapestry, call for vigilance. In a world of vertical cities and horizontal morals, return to simplicity: fast Mondays and Thursdays, give zakat, and seek forgiveness. The Prophet (peace be upon him) said, "Whoever guarantees me what is between his jaws and what is between his legs, I guarantee him Paradise" (Sahih Bukhari)—a timeless shield.

Chapter 10: More Minor Signs – Transformations in Time, Society, and Nature

The minor signs extend to temporal shifts, human behaviors, and natural phenomena, each a thread in the divine countdown. These are not random; they interweave to signal the Hour's approach, as the Prophet (peace be upon him) detailed in extended narrations (Sahih Muslim).

1- The Shrinking of Time and Proximity of Markets: Days feel shorter, tasks endless—a compression of barakah (blessing). "Time will contract so that a year feels like a month" (Sahih Bukhari). In 2025, with 24/7 economies and AI speeding workflows, yet burnout rising, this resonates. Markets cluster, trade booms: "The Hour will not come until wealth multiplies" (Sahih Bukhari), evident in e-commerce giants like Amazon dominating global bazaars.

2- Appearance of Shirk, Trade Expansion, and Earthly Calamities: Hidden polytheism (shirk khafi) creeps in—superstitions, nationalism over tawhid. Trade flourishes, but earthquakes (zalazil), sinkings, and transformations abound: "The earth will swallow people" (Sahih Muslim). Recent quakes in Turkey (2023) and volcanic activity echo this; the Prophet (peace be upon him) said, "Earthquakes will increase" (Sunan Abi Dawud). Respond with sadaqah jariyah to mitigate divine wrath.

3- Rise of the Lowly, Selective Greetings, and the Clothed Yet Naked: The base ascend, leaders from shepherds (Sahih Bukhari)—seen in populist rises. Salam becomes rare, offered only to known faces amid distrust. Women "clothed yet naked" (Sunan Ibn Majah)—modest in attire but immodest in behavior—mirrors fashion trends blending hijab with revealing cuts. Cars symbolize speed: "The Hour comes when feet move faster than light" (metaphorical for rapid transit).

4- True Dreams, Spread of Writing, and Crescent Expansion: Believers' dreams become prophetic (Sahih Bukhari), a gift amid deception. Pens (knowledge) proliferate, yet much is futile. The crescent moon appears larger, symbolizing distorted perceptions.

5- Lies in Religion, Demons from the Sea, and Demographic Shifts: Fabrication in faith rises; shayatin emerge from oceans (Sunan Abi Dawud), perhaps metaphor for naval threats or moral floods. Women outnumber men; sudden deaths surge—heart attacks, accidents—as "Plagues will come" (Sahih Bukhari).

6- Hostility, Greening of Arabia, Excessive Rain, and the Euphrates' Gold: Enmity divides peoples; the Peninsula greens with rivers (Sahih Muslim), possibly climate shifts. Rain pours but yields nothing, like barren economies. The Euphrates uncovers gold, sparking greed (Sahih Bukhari)—echoing resource wars.

7- Speaking Animals, Desire for Death, Roman Growth, Constantinople's Fall, Qahtaan's Reign, Madinah's Purification, and the Blessed Wind:

Wonders like animals speaking (metaphorical for signs); believers yearn for death amid fitan. Romans (Western powers) multiply; Constantinople falls (historical, but symbolic for Eastern shifts). Qahtaan's (Arab tribes) brief rule; Madinah expels evil; a wind claims believers' souls gently (Sahih Muslim). Ka'bah's destruction precedes the Hour.

These signs, like puzzle pieces, form a mosaic of warning. In 2025's divided world—AI ethics clashing with spiritual voids—they urge: fortify iman through Quran study, community service, and dua. The Prophet (peace be upon him) said, "Whoever sees these signs should hold fast to his faith" (Musnad Ahmad). As minor signs accumulate, the major ones loom—may Allah protect us.

Chapter 11: The Major Signs of the Hour – Portents of the End

As the minor signs weave a tapestry of gradual decay, the major signs (Al-Ayat al-Kubra) erupt like thunderclaps, heralding the Hour's imminent arrival. These ten cataclysmic events, foretold by the Prophet Muhammad (peace be upon him), mark the final unraveling of creation: "The Hour will not come until... the ten signs appear" (Sahih Muslim). They are not metaphors but literal upheavals, testing the remnants of faith in a world on the brink.In the Quran, Allah teases their scale: "Are they waiting for anything but the Hour to come upon them suddenly? Its signs have already come" (Surah Muhammad 47:18). The Prophet (peace be upon him) listed them: the Dajjal (Antichrist), the descent of Isa ibn Maryam (Jesus, peace be upon him), Ya'juj and Ma'juj (Gog and Magog), three sinkings of the earth, the smoke (Dukhan), the sun rising from the west, the Beast (Dabbah), and a massive fire driving people to the gathering (Sahih Muslim). These signs, occurring in rapid succession, leave no room for doubt or delay.In 2025, with escalating climate disasters, geopolitical flashpoints, and existential threats like AI gone awry, whispers of these signs echo in global discourse. They remind us: when the extraordinary unfolds, only the steadfast prevail. The Prophet (peace be upon him) said, "When these signs appear, the believer will recognize them as I recognize my own camel" (Ibn Hibban)—a call to vigilance. Let us explore each, drawing lessons for our souls amid the storm.

1- The Emergence of Ad-Dajjal (The Deceiver): The Dajjal, a one-eyed liar with immense power, will claim divinity, performing false miracles like bringing rain or reviving the dead (Sahih Muslim). Blind in one eye (symbolizing spiritual blindness), he bears the word "Kafir" on his forehead, visible to believers. His reign of 40 days (one like a year, one like a month, etc.) will test humanity, offering paradise on earth for allegiance.The Prophet (peace be upon him) warned extensively: "There is no prophet but he warned his people about the Dajjal" (Sahih Muslim). In our time, with deepfakes and charismatic leaders peddling utopian lies, the Dajjal's archetype feels prescient—digital messiahs promising salvation through technology, yet leading to tyranny. Protection: recite the first ten verses of Surah Al-Kahf weekly, and seek refuge in Allah. As Isa (peace be upon him) will slay him near Lod (modern Israel), this sign heralds divine intervention.

2- The Descent of Isa ibn Maryam (Jesus, Peace Be Upon Him): Following the Dajjal's chaos, Isa descends at the white minaret east of Damascus, clad in saffron robes, breaking the cross and abolishing jizyah (Sahih Muslim). He establishes justice, ruling by the Shariah for 40 years, killing pigs and destroying false idols.The Quran affirms: "And there will be none from the People of the Scripture but must surely believe in him before his death" (Surah An-Nisa 4:159). In 2025's interfaith tensions and messianic cults,

Isa's return symbolizes truth's triumph over deception. Believers await him with hope, praying for his era of peace—a brief golden age before further trials.

3- Ya'juj and Ma'juj (Gog and Magog): Released from their barrier (built by Dhul-Qarnayn, Surah Al-Kahf 18:93-98), these barbaric hordes swarm the earth, drinking lakes dry and causing devastation (Sahih Bukhari). Their numbers overwhelm, like "waves of the sea."The Prophet (peace be upon him) described: "They will drink the Sea of Galilee in one gulp" (Sahih Muslim). Interpreted as ancient tribes or modern hordes (perhaps Eastern powers in end-times narratives), they represent unchecked chaos. In today's migrations and conflicts, this sign urges fortitude—Allah will destroy them via a plague, affirming His sovereignty.

4- The Three Earth Sinkings: Three massive landslides—one in the East, one in the West, one on the Arabian Peninsula—swallow armies and lands (Sahih Muslim). These cataclysms, like divine reclamations, signal creation's collapse. Echoing 2025's seismic activities and sinkholes from climate change, they remind: the earth, once a cradle, becomes a grave. The Prophet (peace be upon him) said, "The earth will throw out its treasures" (Sunan Abi Dawud)—a prelude to the Hour.

5- The Smoke (Ad-Dukhan): A thick fog engulfs the world for 40 days, causing mild affliction to believers but death to disbelievers (Sahih Muslim). The Quran foretells: "Then watch for the Day when the sky will bring a visible smoke" (Surah Ad-Dukhan 44:10).In an age of wildfires and pollution, this sign evokes apocalyptic haze—yet it's supernatural, a final mercy call. Protection: faith shields, as the Prophet (peace be upon him) recited Surah Ad-Dukhan for refuge.

6- The Sun Rising from the West: The sun reverses its course, nullifying repentance thereafter (Sahih Bukhari). This cosmic inversion shatters natural laws, proving Allah's command.Amid 2025's solar anomalies and conspiracy theories, it symbolizes irreversible choices—once the door closes, deeds are sealed. The Prophet (peace be upon him) said, "The Hour will not come until the sun rises from the west, and when it does, faith will not benefit those who did not believe before" (Sahih Bukhari).

7' The Beast of the Earth (Dabbat al-Ard): A creature emerges, speaking to humanity, marking believers' faces with light and disbelievers with darkness (Sahih Muslim). The Quran hints: "And when the word befalls them, We will bring forth for them a creature from the earth speaking to them that the people were not certain in Our verses" (Surah An-Naml 27:82).In a biotech era of genetic wonders, this beast—perhaps symbolic of truth's emergence—exposes hidden hearts. It concludes the signs, ushering the final trumpet.

8- The Massive Fire: A blaze from Yemen drives survivors to the gathering site on the bare plain of Sham (Sahih Muslim), herding like camels.

These major signs, unfolding in sequence, culminate creation's drama. In 2025's fragile world, they inspire awe: prepare now, for delay has no place. The Prophet (peace be upon him) urged dua for witnessing them in faith (Tirmidhi). May Allah make us among the protected.

Chapter 12: The Hour (As-Sa'ah) – The Trumpet and Its Echoes

The Hour dawns with the blast of the Trumpet (As-Sur), a sound that rends the heavens and shatters the earth, ushering universal annihilation. The angel Israfil, poised with lips to the horn, awaits Allah's command: "And the Trumpet will be blown, and whoever is in the heavens and whoever is on the earth will fall dead except whom Allah wills" (Surah Az-Zumar 39:68). This is the first blast (Nafkhat al-Faza'), fainting all creation in terror.The Prophet (peace be upon him) described: "The sun will rise from the west, the beast will speak, and then the Trumpet will be blown" (Sahih Bukhari). Time suspends; mountains pulverize, oceans boil, stars scatter (Surah At-Takwir 81:1-6). In

2025, with nuclear shadows and cosmic threats, this evokes ultimate vulnerability—yet for believers, it's liberation from dunya's burdens.When is it blown? Only Allah knows: "They ask you about the Hour: when is its arrival? Say, 'Its knowledge is only with my Lord'" (Surah Al-A'raf 7:187). Signs precede, but the exact moment remains hidden, a test of patience.Exceptions: Eight angels bear the Throne (Surah Al-Haqqah 69:17), and perhaps prophets or martyrs (debated among scholars). The second blast (Nafkhat al-Ba'ath) resurrects all forty years later (Sunan Abi Dawud), souls returning to reformed bodies.Events cascade: birds hover motionless, wild beasts mingle unafraid (Surah At-Takwir 81:5), pregnant women miscarry from shock. The disbeliever cries, "Woe to us! Who has raised us from our sleeping place?" (Surah Ya-Sin 36:52). Believers rejoice in reunion. This Hour, terrifying yet just, levels all—preparing us for accountability.

Chapter 13: Resurrection (Al-Ba'ath) – The Awakening of Souls

Resurrection is creation's rebirth, souls reunited with bodies in a spectacle of divine power. The Trumpet's second blast revives all: "And the Horn will be blown, and behold! From the graves to their Lord they will rush" (Surah Ya-Sin 36:51). Allah commands, "Be," and it is (Surah Al-Baqarah 2:117)—a miracle eclipsing the first creation.How does it occur? The earth quakes violently: "When the earth is shaken with its [final] earthquake... that Day, it will report its news" (Surah Az-Zalzalah 99:1-4). Graves split, bodies emerge—reformed from dust, even if scattered or devoured (Sahih Bukhari). The Prophet (peace be upon him) said, "Allah will reassemble the body from its tailbone (ajb adhdhanab), the seed of resurrection" (Sahih Muslim).Who rises first? The Prophet (peace be upon him): "I will be the first to be resurrected, then Abu Bakr, then Umar" (Sunan Abi Dawud). Prophets and martyrs follow, a procession of honor.Allah assembles humanity on Al-Mahshar, a vast white plain in the barren valley of Juruf (near Jerusalem), enduring 50,000 years under scorching sun (Surah Al-Ma'arij 70:4). Bodies vary: believers youthful (33 years, Sahih Bukhari), disbelievers deformed by sins.Dressed first: Believers in sirwal (undergarments) of Paradise silk (Sahih Bukhari). Conditions: Naked, barefoot, uncircumcised (Sunan Ibn Majah), sweating per deeds—some to ankles, others drowning (Sahih Bukhari).This resurrection, from dust to judgment, affirms justice: no soul wronged. In 2025's inequalities, it promises equity—deeds, not status, prevail. Prepare: "Every soul will come pledging itself" (Surah Al-Isra 17:34). May Allah resurrect us among the righteous.

Chapter 14: The Day of Judgment (Yawm al-Qiyamah) – The Ultimate Reckoning

The Day of Judgment—Yawm al-Qiyamah—is the climax of human history, a day of unparalleled magnitude where every secret is unveiled, every deed weighed, and every soul held accountable. The Quran devotes over one-third of its verses to this event, emphasizing its inevitability and terror: "O mankind, fear your Lord. Indeed, the earthquake of the Hour is a terrible thing" (Surah Al-Hajj 22:1). It is the fulfillment of divine justice, where oppression ends, truth triumphs, and Allah's promise manifests: "So today no soul will be wronged in anything, and you will not be recompensed except for what you used to do" (Surah Ya-Sin

36:54).Names abound for this day, each evoking its facets: Yawm al-Fasl (Day of Separation, Surah Al-Mursalat 77:13), Yawm al-Hisab (Day of Reckoning, Surah Ghafir 40:27), Yawm al-Din (Day of Recompense, Surah Al-Fajr 89:22), and Yawm al-Hasrah (Day of Regret, Surah Maryam 19:39). The Prophet Muhammad (peace be upon him) called it "the day longer than fifty thousand years" (Surah Al-Ma'arij 70:4), a duration felt subjectively—bliss for the righteous, eternity for the wicked.Descriptions paint a scene of cosmic upheaval: the sun folds up, stars scatter, mountains crumble like wool (Surah At-Takwir 81:1-6), and the heavens split asunder (Surah Al-Infitar 82:1). Humanity, resurrected and assembled on the vast plain of Al-Mahshar, stands barefoot and naked under a sun drawn near (Surah Al-Qari'ah 101:5-9). Disbelievers wail in despair: "Our Lord, remove us [from this]; we will do righteous work" (Surah Fatir 35:37), but the door to deeds slams shut.For the disbeliever, it is catastrophe: faces blackened, garments torn, wailing like howling camels (Surah Abasa 80:37-41). They plead with believers for water or intercession, but find none (Surah Al-Mu'minun 23:106-108). The hypocrite, outwardly pious, is exposed: "On the Day when the hypocrite's secrets are revealed" (Surah At-Tawbah 9:94). Sinners among Muslims tremble, hoping for mercy, yet burdened by scales tipping against them.The righteous, however, stand serene: faces radiant, clothed in silken dignity (Surah Al-Insan 76:9-12). They rejoice in foretold glad tidings, their deeds a luminous shield. Rules govern: no intercession without permission (Surah An-Najm 53:26), scales balanced precisely (Surah Al-Anbiya 21:47), and books of deeds distributed—right hands for the successful, left or behind backs for the doomed (Surah Al-Inshiqaq 84:7-12).Questioning begins: "About the favors [upon you], what did you deny?" (Surah Ar-Rahman 55:13). Prophets witness for their nations (Surah Al-Ma'idah 5:109), and even limbs testify (Surah Ya-Sin 36:65). Events unfold in sequence: the Sirat bridge, thinner than hair and sharper than sword, crossed by the faithful in moments, while others plummet (Sahih Bukhari). In 2025's world of fleeting justice—corrupt trials, biased algorithms—this Day promises perfect equity, where no bribe sways the Judge.The importance? It motivates: live as if every act is recorded, for "No soul knows what has been hidden for them of comfort for eyes as reward for what they used to do" (Surah As-Sajdah 32:17). Outline: assembly, questioning, scales, Sirat, then entry to abodes eternal.

Chapter 15: Hellfire (Jahannam) – The Abode of Torment

Hellfire—Jahannam—is the ultimate deterrent, a realm of unrelenting anguish reserved for those who rejected truth or oppressed in life. The Quran depicts it vividly: "Fear the Fire whose fuel is men and stones, prepared for the disbelievers" (Surah Al-Baqarah 2:24). Its seven gates lead to layers of escalating horror, guarded by angels stern (Surah Al-Hijr 15:44).Descriptions evoke dread: boiling water scalds faces (Surah Al-Kahf 18:29), thorny fruits choke the damned (Surah Ad-Dukhan 44:43-46), and chains bind the arrogant (Surah Al-Insan 76:4). Flames leap like yellow camels (Surah Al-Haqqah 69:30-32), and the tree of Zaqqum pierces bellies like devils' heads (Surah As-Saffat

37:62-68). Punishments tailor to sins: adulterers boiled in pus (Sahih Bukhari), usurers' flesh raked by fire (Sunan Abi Dawud), backbiters' mouths torn (Tirmidhi).Eternal torment awaits the defiant: Pharaoh, Abu Lahab, disbelievers who mocked prophets (Surah Al-Muddaththir 74:26-30). Temporary for sinful Muslims, purified before Paradise (Sahih Muslim). The majority? Women and the weak prevail in salvation, but Hell's population swells with rejectors (Sahih Bukhari).In 2025's moral relativism—where vice is normalized via apps and media—this warns: fire's fuel is not wood, but human folly. The Prophet (peace be upon him) said, "Hell is veiled by desires, and Paradise by hardships" (Sahih Bukhari). Escape: tawbah, sadaqah, Quran recitation—shields against the blaze.

Chapter 16: Paradise (Jannah) – The Gardens of Eternal Bliss

Paradise—Jannah—is the crown jewel of faith, a realm of unimaginable delight where "no fatigue will touch them, nor will they [ever] be removed from there" (Surah Al-Hijr 15:48). Its eight gates open to rivers of milk, honey, wine, and water (Surah Muhammad 47:15), palaces of gold and silver, and companions pure (Surah Ar-Rahman 55:56-78).Gates include Ar-Rayyan for fasters, Bab al-Jihad for warriors of faith (Sahih Bukhari). How many enter? A vast multitude: "My Ummah will enter in groups" (Sahih Muslim), with 99/100 of creation in Jannah (Sunan Abi Dawud). The Sirat purifies, then entry to delights: houris (companions) unmatched in beauty (Surah Ar-Rahman 55:70), fruits unending (Surah Al-Waqi'ah 56:28-33).Why eat in Jannah? For joy, not need—meals enhance bliss (Tirmidhi). Marital reunions: righteous spouses together (Sahih Bukhari). Gold and silver adorn, but hearts purified (Surah Az-Zukhruf 43:71). Conversations with Hell's dwellers highlight mercy (Sahih Muslim); worship is tasbih in ecstasy (Surah Al-Fajr 89:27-30).The marketplace trades sights for deeds (Ibn Majah); latecomers arrive to full joy (Sahih Bukhari). Jannah's obstacles? Desires veil it (Sahih Muslim); heirs from Hell's remnants (Tirmidhi). Majority: the weak and oppressed (Sahih Bukhari). Gender balance? More women, yet equality in reward (debated, but mercy prevails). Believers' children enter (Sahih Bukhari); non-believers' do not. Glad tidings for the steadfast (Surah Yunus 10:64).Jannah vs. dunya: pure vs. contaminated (Surah Al-Insan 76:21). Dunya temporary, Jannah eternal—enjoy without excess. Final note: Adam's stature (60 cubits, Sahih Bukhari), age 33 upon entry (Tirmidhi), no sleep (continuous delight). Bounties unseen: "No soul knows what is kept hidden for them of joy as a reward" (Surah As-Sajdah 32:17). A primitive tribe couldn't grasp snow; likewise, Jannah defies imagination. No filth, kingship in grace (Surah Al-Insan 76:20).

Conclusion: A Call to Eternal Readiness

As we conclude this eternal journey, let the Hereafter not remain a distant echo but a living compass. From dunya's fleeting train to the grave's solitude, the Hour's signs, Judgment's scales, Hell's blaze, and Paradise's gardens, every chapter whispers: prepare now. The Prophet (peace be upon him) said, "The believer's affair is amazing—all is good for him" (Sahih Muslim). In trials, patience; in ease, gratitude.In 2025's tempests—pandemics lingering, economies fracturing, faiths tested—hold to the rope of Allah. Recite Quran nightly, give sadaqah daily, seek forgiveness in sujud. Visit graves, ponder signs, and dua: "O Allah, make the Hereafter our chief concern, and make us among those who recognize Your signs."May this book ignite a flame in your heart, guiding you to Jannah's gates. For the smart soul subdues desires today for eternal triumph tomorrow. Wa sallallahu ala sayyidina Muhammad.

References

1- Quran: All cited surahs from the Uthmani script (e.g., Al-Hajj 22:1, Ya-Sin 36:54, Al-Ankabut 29:57, etc.).

2- Hadith Collections: Sahih Bukhari (e.g., grave as garden/pit, Sirat bridge); Sahih Muslim (major signs, deeds after death); Sunan Abi Dawud (questioning in grave, first resurrected); Sunan Tirmidhi (dhikr al-mawt, Surah Al-Mulk); Sunan Ibn Majah (eternal torment, age in Jannah); Musnad Ahmad (grave's light); Ibn Hibban (life's days); Tabarani (remembering death 20 times).

3- Additional Sources: Tafsir Ibn Kathir (for sign interpretations); Ibn al-Qayyim's Zad al-Ma'ad (on preparation for Hereafter).